When We Were Kids

by

Hank Stohl

1663 LIBERTY DRIVE, SUITE 200
BLOOMINGTON, INDIANA 47403
(800) 839-8640
WWW.AUTHORHOUSE.COM

© 2005 Hank Stohl. All Rights Reserved.

No part of this book may be reproduced, stored in a retrieval system, or transmitted by any means without the written permission of the author.

First published by AuthorHouse 12/13/04

ISBN: 1-4184-9621-9 (sc)

Library of Congress Control Number: 2004195070

Printed in the United States of America
Bloomington, Indiana

This book is printed on acid-free paper.

Dear Reader

The most difficult task in compiling this Compendium was trying to include most, if not all, every Children's TV Personality in Pittsburgh Television in the Late Fifties and early sixties. What I call our Golden age in Kid's TV.

I found it impossible to include everyone.

Most of their recorded history is gone. Erased. Trashed. Recorded history is gone. Stations, and their lack of imagination, tossed out Tapes and films and volumes of recorded TV History. There are no tapes. No Film. Remember, it was live TV. Stations found it not practical to store volumes of TV History. *(How great it would be to see some of those TV shows today)*

Their images, however, are indelibly etched in the minds of the kids who watched. I realize that many names and shows have been omitted. It was impossible to track down those not included. With deep apologies to them, We hope you enjoy reading about some of these few.

Enjoy!!!

Hank Stohl   © 2004

Special Thanks to: Jean Connelly, David Newell of Family Communication, Dolores Ellenberg, VP Development of the Carnegie Museum of Pittsburgh. And to all those included in this publication, who went to their own personal files to contribute Photos and Material.

The Intersection
PO BOX 827
115 Seventh Ave.,
McKeesport, Pa. 15134
412-678-6948

Founded in 1972 by the Sisters of Mercy, The Intersection is known as an inter-denominational Community Center.

The services include on-site Meal Program food pantry club, Distribution of clothing, Assistance in locating Temporary Housing, also the distribution of Clothing, household goods and furniture.

The Intersection is housed in the former Reformed Hungarian Church. In 1992 The Sisters of Mercy bought the building. After repairs and Grants from the Pittsburgh Foundation and the City of McKeesport, The Intersection incorporated, and began it's work in the area:

The on-site Program provides a hot midday meal to those who are hungry. In the year 2002, a Total of 15,249 meals were served by representatives of various churches in the area and by intersection volunteers.

During 1994, the Intersection initiated on site-health services. operation Safety Net (OSN) Mercy Hospital provides a physician and Nurse each Week, along with a broad range of support services – free chest X-rays. influenza vaccines and access to eye and dental care. The food is provided by the greater Pittsburgh food bank and the Emergency food assistance Program.

The Intersection continues to be known as an inter-denominational Community Center, and ecumenical place of sharing where persons can relax and interact in a peaceful environment.

for this reason, After printing costs and taxes, all author profits from this publication <u>are donated to The Intersection.</u>

Table of Contents

Ida Mae & Happy 1
Capn' Jim 7
Josey Carey 11
Indian Mary (Johnny Costa) 17
Sterling Yates 21
Knish 27
Rodney 31
Connie 35
Cuzzin 39
MISS "B" 43
Kay-Dee Kartoons 49
Don Riggs (Bwana Don) 57
The Big Adventure 65
Mitzi's Kiddie Castle (Mitzie Steiner) 73
Paul Shannon (Adventure Time) 79
Fred Rogers 89
Don Brockett (Chef Brockett) 95
David Newell (Mr. McFeeley) 101
Bob Trow 107
Ricki & Copper (Ricki Wertz) 113
Miss Janey Vance 121
Joe Negri (Handyman Negri) 125
Children's Favorites on WTAE 131
Nickelodeon 139

Ida Mae & Happy

HAPPY's PARTY

Happy's Party was the very first Local Children's Program in Pittsburgh, It was created and hosted by Ida Mae Stilley. A matronly Dental Hygienist for the Pittsburgh Schools.

Her Program promoted good oral health care with her hand Puppet, Happy, who nestled in Ida Mae's folded arm. Happy never spoke. He whispered into Ida Mae's ear – Ida would then repeat what Happy said to her.

It played on WDTV, Channel 3 for fifteen minutes on a Saturday morning, from 10:45 until 11:00 AM. When the station became KDKA-TV, the program was sponsored by the Fort Pitt Tomato Company, and then the Florida Citrus Commission.

Her signature sign-off, "Remember, Happy loves you" became a local quote...and influenced many children's programs later.

Mr. and Mrs. Happy is what the puppy's guardians, Ida Mae and Thomas Maher, often are called.

Pert Pup: Here's "Happy", doing a chore with the help of his originator, Ida May Stilley.

Photo Courtesy: Carnegie Library

Capn' Jim

Cap'n Jim on the Tug, Nancy B.

Cap'n Jim hosted cartoons on WIIC-TV, in the early sixties --- No Photos were found of Ted Echman, who reportedly died in 1973.

Josey Carey

Josie Carey

Josey Carey was a pioneer in Public Television, Having Appeared on the very first broadcast on WQED-TV in April of 1954.

Working with Fred Rogers, She created and starred in an hour long Children's Program, entitled, The Children's corner" Seen daily for seven years. It was also syndicated on National education and on NBC.

She then went to KDKA-TV on such programs as Josie' Story land and Josie's World. Other notable programs were "Funsville", "Wingding" with Johnny Costa and Sterling Yates.

Her awards include The Sylvania Award for best children's Program, Page one award from the newspaper Guild, TV radio magazine award and the prized Q award for outstanding contributions to educational Television. Josie also did a Sunday Radio show on KDKA Radio and "Josie's Attic" on WQEX.

Josie had enjoyed Appearing and directing scores of Productions at Local theaters for the past ten years.

Josie Carey Died in June of 2004.

Complications from a fall in her home contributed to her death.. a Bright and shining star had been unexpectedly extinguished.

Josie Carey and Daniel Tiger
Photo Courtesy: Family Communications

When We Were Kids

Photo Courtesy: Family Communications

Indian Mary
(Johnny Costa)

Indian Mary: Johnny Costa On Josey Carey's "Funsville"

The musical inserts and accompaniment was handled by the very talented Johnny Costa. Rather than just sit and play, It was decided that the music be handled by a Character named Indian Mary. Who, incidentally, chomped on a cigar.. That was "Indian Mary". Where the name came from, as well as the idea came from is lost forever...obviously, Smoking on a children's Program would not be acceptable today, But Late fifties--- Why not? Johnny went on to become the Musical Director of Mr. Roger's Neighborhood.

Hank Stohl

Johnny Costa as Indian Mary
Photo Courtesy: Carnegie Museum Library

Sterling Yates

Sterling Yates

Sterling was a versatile and talented performer, He appeared on "Cordic and Company" on KDKA radio, in a variety of character roles.

On "Funsville" with Josie Carey, Sterling was "Mr. Cupples", and Mr. Wrinkle", Other character creations were Fester Clodworthy and Snark Dutry, a dysfunctional and scrambled Astronaut. He was a music graduate of Carnegie Tech in 1951, and was proficient on Sax, Clarinet & oboe. He often performed with the Pittsburgh Symphony and Opera, He also starred in stage productions at the Pittsburgh Playhouse. An NBC executive heard Sterling on radio, and offered him work on WNBC in New York City in 1966.

In 1967, at forty years of age, he suffered a stroke and aneurysm, After a remarkable recovery, and therapy, Sterling as able to perform in national Commercials. He was diagnosed with throat cancer, and the man of many talents and voices was forced into early retirement. Sterling died in 1991 of an apparent heart Attack after returning to Pittsburgh.

Hank Stohl with Sterling Yates at Allegheny County Airport getting a brief lesson in weather at DeNardo-McFarland Weather headquarters. Among Sterling's versatility was his ability to do a weather show on KDKA-TV.
Photo courtesy KDKA-TV

When We Were Kids

STERLING YATES as SNARK DUTRY
Photo Courtesy: Carnegie Museum Library

STERLING YATES
Photo Courtesy: Rogers Professional Registry

KNISH

Knish Was conceived on a Weekend Before a Planned Audition on WDTV (Dumont) In Pittsburgh in 1952. He made his first appearance on "Mitzie's Kiddie Kastle." Mitzie Called him *"Knish"*. Hank agreed to the name change. He conceded that as it was her show, he consented to the name change from "Clarence" to Knish.

Hank Stohl had some experience with puppets in Dayton, Ohio, at WLW-D and was asked if he would bring his Puppets in for a "Look see" and possible appearance on Mitzie's show. Only problem was, there were none. They all were still in Dayton, as the property of that Station. That weekend, He worked on Making puppets for Mitzie's show. A Darning egg and Rug Yarn were the answer. Knish was created, and showed up on Monday for his Audition. He was immediately accepted as a participating cast member. Knish then went on to become a regular on the popular "Bill Brant show". From there, KNISH won a chance to host his own Program with cartoons and guests; A show that lasted from 1952 until Hank went to New York City in 1964, after successful runs on KDKA-TV and WTAE-TV in Pittsburgh. Knish wowed New York audiences by beating all competition: Knish beat Soupy Sales, Chuck McCann and Sandy Becker on WPIX, New York in the ratings.

In 1968, Hand decided to retire Knish and Rodney, moving to California in that year to pursue an acting career, appearing in many Series and films. Hank predicted that the Live & local Children's show Phenomena would end, and there would be no demand for his services. He was right. Local Children's programs ended with the invasion of slick film and taped shows from Hollywood and New York with fantastic budgets. Hank recalled that the budget for his daily show was Twenty dollars a week.

Knish was conceived with the deliberate intent as a mischievous boy with hair in his face, always challenging his Mentor, "Rodney. Hank Stohl admits that the cartoon character, "Hairless Joe" in "Al Capp's "Lil Abner' influenced the design of "Knish."

RODNEY

Rodney Nugent Buster Hackenflash III

was the Perfect Foil for KNISH. He was the mentor, Disciplinarian, Teacher, an Father figure to Knish. He Scolded, Taught & instructed – and tried to keep Knish in line.. (Hardly ever successfully.)

He was Modeled in demeanor and manner of W.C. Fields.. Somewhat of a martinet, Rodney was the perfect foil and straight man for knish and his antics. His lessons were always good and honest, Never devious or wrong. He was honest, always frustrated by Knish's Antics. But always respected by Knish.

They were good friends... Despite the many harmless pranks played on him by Knish. His background was that of an older Vaudevillian and actor, fond of Shakespeare and the *"boards" on one..* He knew the stage well, and tried to impart this experience to Knish. *(A never ending instruction course)* always questioned by Knish.

His Full name was Rodney Nugent Buster Hackenflash the Third.. Where that came from, God only knows. His outfit as tailored and designed, sewn by Margo Lovelace of Pittsburgh Puppet Theatre fame.

Originally named Miss Bakerville", Hank changed her name to "Miss B". Parent's complained that Children couldn't pronounce, *Miss Baskerville"*. They butchered the name and it bordered on profanity. *let your imagination figure it out..* So "Miss B' it was.

She was the Madame Dumont of the KNISH cast, Knew one—*only* **one** song and imagined herself as an Operatic diva.. Her *one* song was... "Only a bird in a gilded cage..."

She was voiced by Hank Stohl because he only knew One song.. and also admits to not being able to carry a tune..

Voice by Hank Stohl

CONNIE

Every boy has a dog. Knish had "Connie."

Connie originally Constructed as a Donkey by Connie Hula, Hank simply took the wire Stiffeners from his ears, and behold: *"It's now a dog"*.

Connie could Rollover, Count to three, Sit, and lay down.

and that's all.

Connie used to love to lick Knish's face and never obey knish. But that was okay. They were inseparable.

Barked and growled by Hank Stohl.

CUZZIN

CUZZIN Resembled Knish. Long unkempt Hair, Huge nose.. *(It (ran in the family.* He was an occasional contributor to the many Situations and antics of the regular cast. He was lazy, always tired, and constantly taking naps on stage, much to the chagrin of Knish, Connie and Rodney. He frequently Fell asleep in the middle of conversations with Knish Voiced by his manipulator: Hank Stohl.

MISS "B"

Hank Stohl

Hank began his career in radio and experimental Television as early as 1948 In Cincinnati, Ohio and Pittsburgh, Pennsylvania. Then to New York City to where he Appeared in his highly successful children's TV Program, He is best remembered as the creator Knish, Rodney & Connie who are now residing at the Heinz History Center in Pittsburgh.

As Creative director of his own Creative company He also created several Award winning radio and TV commercials as producer and writer for several National Accounts, Camel Cigarettes, International Industries, The island nation of Bermuda and Pepsi-West and Taco-Bell.

Hank also appeared in several series, and feature films, "Rockford files", "Highway to heaven", and "six million dollar man", Along with appearances on "Days of our lives", and the Guiding light". His most recent film was "Diabolique' which starred Sharon Stone and Kathy Bates.

He is a published playwright And his two act comedy, "Lie a little" enjoyed great reviews while a member of the famed Masquers Club in Hollywood. Several one act plays have been published and produced Off-Off Broadway in New York. Hank is married to Anita Heh, former staff member of the Pittsburgh Playhouse and musical comedy performer. They live in Stratford, Connecticut.

Hank Stohl: Popeye and Knish

Kay-Dee Kartoons

Kay-Dee Kartoons was a cartoon show with a "live" wraparound provided by Hank Stohl and his Puppets, Knish, Rodney and Connie. It proved an immensely popular program and began its long run in October of 1955. It was on from 12:15 pm until 12:30 pm - Monday through Friday. The ideal time for children at lunchtime *(When kids used to come home from school for lunch.)*

Photo Courtesy: KDKA-TV

Hank Stohl

Hank Goes Western

HANK STOHL TOOK a week off from his duties as morning wakeup and afternoon kiddies' specialist with WTAE several weeks ago to return to Hollywood and make his second appearance with Chuck Connors in "Rifleman," seen Tuesdays at 8 p. m. on Channels 4 and 10.

Stohl plays a nasty bad man and Connors eventually finishes him off in the show which will be seen in the early spring. Here are advance glimpses of Hank and Chuck on set in Hollywood.

After he's taken care of the villainous Stohl, Connors records him for posterity with the help of young Johnny Crawford, who's about to commit a petty injustice.

While Stohl bravely hams it up for the rolling camera, hero Chuck Connors sets out to finish him off during filming of "Rifleman" episode to be seen on Channels 4, 10.

When We Were Kids

1959

Hank Stohl

Hank Stohl
Photo Courtesy: Hank Stohl

When We Were Kids

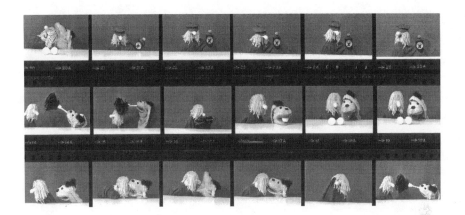

Don Riggs
(Bwana Don)

Don Riggs
Don Riggs, (Bwana Don)

For seven Years, Don Held the children of Pittsburgh Spellbound with his Saturday Morning Jungle Adventure program, "Safari"" His guests ranged from Big game handlers to Big Game - Chimpanzees, Mountain Lions and a variety of Snakes and reptiles were all part of his program. sometimes the visiting kids would make their entrances on a tarzan like rope swing. The practice, however, was discontinued when one child couldn't hold on for his entire swing --. He brought Children and Animals together in a version of Wild Kingdom. On Safari, Many Tarzan Films were Shown. Occasionally, His puppet Friend, "Willie" the pesky duck, manipulated and voiced by Don would interject his brand of humor into the program. After seven successful years as host of 'Safari", Don went on to host WPXI's *'starting Today'"* An Avid Aviation enthusiast and pilot, Don Also was President of the Pittsburgh, Aero Club, One of Aviation's oldest Aero *Organizations*. He was also in great demand as narrator at air shows both regionally and Nationally.

A native of Ohio, Don and his family can trace a strong association back to the Wright Brothers of Dayton, Ohio. Willie - Pittsburgh's Pesky puppet created lots of memories for all who enjoy the fun of puppets, especially rubber Ducks.

Regular (yearly) safari guest
KDKA-TV Photo
by JIM STARK

"Scratch My Back" "Thomas John" star of Noell's Ark menagerie, Sarasota. 1964

Hank Stohl

DON RIGGS
Cartoon Colorama With Willie

Saturday 1 P.M.   Sunday 9 A.M.

Hank Stohl

The Big Adventure

The Big Adventure

Was on the air Daily from 4:45 to 6:45 Pm. It replaced the very popular "Buzz and Bill"" variety and musical program.

It began with Cartoons hosted by Knish & Rodney, then a full length adventure feature, interspersed with skits and comedy bits in an adventure flavor suggested by the content and plot of the full length film.

It ran successfully on KDKA-TV for three years.

The format was modeled after a similar program at KDKA's sister station in Cleveland,

"The Big Adventure" Set
with Host Hank Stohl
4:45-6:45 Daily on KDKA-TV

Big Adventure insert page

Many visiting Stars guested on Hank Stohl's *Big Adventure* program; Sammy Davis Jr. Jack Lemon and chuck Connors to name but a few – It was during a visit with Chuck Connors, publicizing his soon to be released show, entitled, "Rifleman," That Chuck invited Hank to California to appear in a small role on his show, The episode was entitled "Ordeal" and was nominated for an Emmy. that year.

When We Were Kids

Photo courtesy KDKA-TV

'WHAT'S UP, JERRY?' Hank Stohl, host of Channel 2's "Big Adventure," talks things over with Jerry, who appeared as guest on the KDKA-TV show.

When We Were Kids

Hank goes to the moon...with Johnny Skyrocket on "The Big Adventure" on KDKA-TV July, 1958 during "A History of Flight Celebration".

Mitzi's Kiddie Castle
(Mitzie Steiner)

Mitzie's Kiddie Castle

One of WDTV's early Children's TV shows, featured Mitzi Steiner and Hank Stohl and was seen Sundays 12:30 P.M. And was sponsored by Gold Banner bread. A bearded Hank Stohl, appeared as Merlin, The Magician – Merlin was soon replaced by Knish – as one of the featured Characters.

This was an ad seen in TV Dial – January of 1953.

The very Talented and vivacious Mitzi Steiner Changed her professional name to Mitzi McCall, went on to California, appearing on and writing several popular TV shows, with her writer husband, Steve Brill.

Hank Stohl

kiddie castle

Featuring
Mitzi Steiner and Hank Stohl
With Puppets, Songs and Stories

SUNDAYS 12:30 P. M.

Brought to you by
GOLD BANNER BREAD

WDTV Pittsburgh's First Television Station

When We Were Kids

By BILL ADLER

Ray Scott

Harold Lund

Carole Mansfield

Ray Scott and Bob Prince both have package sports shows they're working on . . . The *Post-Gazette* staff is still laughing at Cy Hungerford's winding up the lone winner the night *Guest to Ghost* had an all-*PG* panel. Cy's the worst speller in the editorial room . . . The WDTV gang is drooling at Bossman Harold Lund's sun-tan, the Florida variety. He was there over the holidays. Next big trip for Lund: Mexico City in April as a delegate to the Variety Club convention.

* * *

Mike Mazurki, of *Guys and Dolls* at the Nixon, was a professional wrestler before he smelled greasepaint for the first time in 1941. When teevee put the mastodons back in business, Mazurki was offered a fabulous deal to rejoin the grunters-and-groaners but turned it down. He says acting's much easier and in the long run pays just as well . . . Slim Bryant wouldn't mind if his brother Loppy gave him some of his excess weight. Loppy probably wouldn't mind either.

* * *

The Stanley Theater still can't understand Billy Eckstine's poor business. He's box-office dynamite everywhere . . . WCAE and the Matta outfit just got their applications for Channel 4 in Irwin under the wire. Looked for a time like KQV might grab the license by default . . . Overheard along the night-club belt: "Some morning I'm going to stay up late enough to catch Dave Garroway."

* * *

It's beginning to look as if fall may be the earliest Channel 2 will be able to move from the Chamber of Commerce Building to the Gateway . . . Carole Mansfield (Mrs. John Cole) has been keeping her finger in the teevee pie in Chicago, where the Coles now live. She's been making a flock of filmed commercial spots for a Windy City outfit . . . Mrs. Dorothy Daniel, the pinch-hitter now for the *Ask the Girls* panelists, is the wife of Royal Daniel, managing editor of the *Sun-Telegraph*.

Paul Shannon
(Adventure Time)

Paul Shannon

Paul Shannon Had an amazing career. He was a local Broadcast legend with accomplishments in Radio & TV that are legion. He began his radio career in 1937 on WWSW", Then on to KDKA radio, for 19 years. He then left KDKA for WTAE-TV where he spent more than 17 years.

His Children's Program." "Adventure Time"" on WTAE-TV ran from 1958 until 1975. He wielded his magic sword, Waving it up, then down to introduce Each Segment of Adventure time". Paul is single handedly Responsible for raising thousands of dollars in backyard Carnivals for victims of Muscular Dystrophy. Paul is largely responsible for reviving the careers of the Three Stooges""", whose films were featured on his show. They reciprocated by offering him a film role in one of their features as wild Bill Hickock – the film was, "The ""Outlaws is coming".

Paul was a total gentleman. He died in Florida at the age of 80, where he retired after a long and distinguished Career in Pittsburgh Broadcasting. A call to WTAE-TV, and Manager, Rick Henry requesting Photos of Paul, could find only two pictures on file.

When We Were kids

Paul Shannon and Nesmo King

Hank Stohl

PAUL SHANNON ... features all the children's favorite comedies and cartoons, plus some very unusual guests on his "Adventure Time" program, weekday evenings at 5:00 P.M. The "3 Stooges" have been an integral part of Paul's show for many years and new characters such as Nosmo King add greatly to the children's enjoyment.

When We Were Kids

wtae-tv's Paul Shannon has helped a decade of kids fight Muscular Dystrophy

Paul Shannon, host of WTAE-TV's "Adventure Time" for 14 years, has grown-up with two generations of young viewers. He has been the most successful host of all children's shows in the Pittsburgh area since he began in 1958. Among his many contributions to youngsters and the community, the most outstanding achievement has been his Backyard Carnivals for Muscular Dystrophy in the Pittsburgh area. On his "Adventure Time" show he asked his kids to hold carnivals at home, with the proceeds to be donated to the Muscular Dystrophy Association of America. Each year, the fund raising has been a great success. In 1962, the first year, Paul's kids got $3,540 together. And this past year, they broke all national records, surpassing all other markets, with a fantastic $103,400! Their ten year total exceeds $400,000. WTAE-TV is proud to have a concerned personality like Paul Shannon on its staff. Because it's this type of individual involvement that makes our comittment to the community a real one.

wtae-tv 4
Pittsburgh, Pa.

WTAE-TV's "ADVENTURE TIME" was hosted by Paul Shannon. The show was on-the-air for fourteen years ... 1958 to 1972.

Hank Stohl

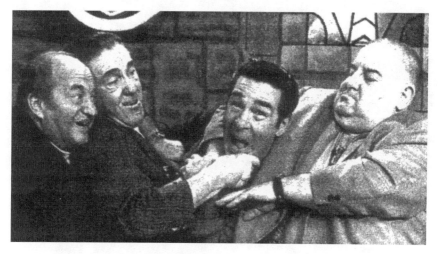

Paul Shannon and the three Stooges Guest on "Adventure Time" on WTAE-TV which debuted in 1958---
Picture Courtesy WTAE-TV

Paul Shannon

Fred Rogers

Fred Rogers
1928-2003

In quoting Betsy Benson, the publisher Editor of Pittsburgh Magazine, ""During his lifetime, Fred Rogers did a remarkable thing, He created a brand new language, comprising of Thousands of simple words That spoke of truth, love and caring."

Fred Rogers did that and more --, He created a television program and characters that will most certainly endure. He was an American institution. He receiving the Presidential Medal of Honor of freedom in July of 2002. Everyone was touched by his Kindness and creative Genius. Fred Rogers began playing the piano when he was only five and wrote more than 200 songs.

Fred Rogers and won An amazing Four Emmy Awards, along with two George Foster Peabody awards for Television Excellence. Fred was also an ordained Minister, graduating from Pittsburgh Theological Seminary. Fred Rogers died in 2003 – Much too soon.

When We Were Kids

FRED ROGERS
www.pbs.org/rogers
www.misterrogers.org

Don Brockett
(Chef Brockett)

Don Brockett
Chef Brockett

One of the more talented and versatile talents ever to grace the Pittsburgh Area Television scene was Don Brockett, who appeared as Chef Brockett on Mr. Rogers Neighborhood as Chef Brockett.

Don, in 1960 formed Brockett productions and created shows for companies, and special events, He is best known for the annual spoof of Pittsburgh, entitled, *"Forbidden Pittsburgh""*

This outrageous and delightful revue wowed audiences Off Broadway and dinner theaters for eleven consecutive years.

He was voted four times as entertainer of the year. In addition to his original stage revues, Don still found time to appear in 34 films.

In ""Forbidden Pittsburgh"", He Appeared as Pittsburgh Mayor, Sophie Masloff, in a delightful parody of her Malapropisms and hairdo, and whiny voice. He wore a pink and black lace strapless evening gown, Sequined scuffs and scads of Rhinestone jewelry. No one in the city administration was safe from his ribbing and brilliantly written and directed parody sketches.

Don died unexpectedly of a heart attack in 1995.

When We Were Kids

Chef Brockett

David Newell
(Mr. McFeeley)

David Newell: Mr. McFeely

When David Newell Appeared on Mr. Rogers Neighborhood, He Played Mr. McFeely, the elderly Neighbor who ran a speedy delivery service. While Visiting, Mr. McFeely often leads to viewing a movie from his extensive movie collection. You might also see anything from a hot-air balloon ride to a flashback to When he was young.

Away from the Character makeup, David Newell assumes many behind the scenes responsibilities for Mr., Rogers Neighborhood. David has been with the series since its inception in 1967. He has been Properties Manager, Associate producer and now is Director of public relations for Family Communications, producers of MISTER ROGERS NEIGHBORHOOD..

David's background include a wide variety of involvement in theater Arts as an actor, Technician, Stage manager and administrator.

David is a native of Pittsburgh, and has worked with the Pittsburgh Playhouse, Civic Light Opera Company and the little Lake Arena Theater. He has also been involved in Theater productions in Los Angeles and Honolulu.

David received his certification in Theater Arts from the Pittsburgh Playhouse and a B.A. in English literature from the university of Pittsburgh. He lives in Pittsburgh with his wife, Nan and three children, Carrie, Taylor and Alexander.

When We Were Kids

Mr. McFeely

www.pbs.org/rogers
www.misterrogers.org

Bob Trow

Bob Trow

Bob Trow was one of the original funny men on Cordic & Co., heard on KDKA in the early Morning. He was Brunhilda among Many other characters featured on the early morning radio Program.

Bob had no formal Music training, but formed many musical groups that performed in the Pittsburgh Area.

He wrote many songs and arrangements. He was also a gifted writer and later worked for the George Hill Advertising agency as creative director, originating many Ad Campaigns for Joseph Horne department Store. Bob was also a gifted artist in Oils & Pastels.

After Cordic left for the West Coast, Bob teamed with Art Pallen on the Early morning Show on KDKA radio. He also

Hank Stohl

appeared with Knish & Company on many industrial parties in the Pittsburgh Area.

he was featured on **Bobdog** and Bob **Troll** with Mr. Rogers' Neighborhood. Bob Trow died of a heart attack at his home in New Alexandria, in October of 1998. He was 72.

MISTER ROGERS' NEIGHBORHOOD®   **Bob Dog**

Ricki & Copper
(Ricki Wertz)

Ricki and Copper

Don Riggs had Willie – Josie Had Tame Tigers – Hank Stohl had Knish – Paul Shannon had Nosmo king.. and Mary had a little Lamb –

Ricki had Copper

Copper was adopted by Ricki and husband Tom from the Animal Shelter – A beautiful Golden retriever who was Ricki's sidekick and TV companion for years. The Ricki and Copper Birthday show was on WTAE-TV and Ricki is quick to admit that Copper was her Co-Star throughout her career, sharing equal billing on every Children's program they appeared on.

Ricki Began her career as a singer and dancer at the Pittsburgh Playhouse and civic light opera in 1952. She became Girl Friday on the Jay Michael's local Bandstand show on WENS, The local UHF Channel in Pittsburgh. Ricki lip-synched the Top record of the week on the show. The director of the show was Tom Borden, who married Ricki in August of 1954, and now live in Irwin, Pa.

Ricki's husband, Tom, Has won many Landscaping awards for his Feng Shui creations.

You probably also remember Ricki as the singing Weather girl on WTAE-TV, at 11 P.M, sponsored by Sealy mattresses. every evening at eleven, She sang the weather forecast, clad in a negligee. needless to say, her fan mail increased ten fold.

Ricki also Appeared as hostess of the very popular Junior High Quiz, sponsored by Pittsburgh National Bank for seventeen years.

After her very successful career in Local Television, Ricki Continued to work in national outreach for Public Television until Retirement in 2000, Ricki also returned to College, earning her MS degree, continuing on to graduate School, and getting her MS degree.

Photo Courtesy Ricki Wertz

Hank Stohl

When We Were Kids

Ricki Wertz and the THREE STOOGES on "Ricky's Comedy Time."
Photo Courtesy: WTAE-TV

Ricki as host of the very popular "Jr. High Quiz"

Miss Janey Vance

Janey Vance

"Bend and Stretch. Reach for the Stars – There goes Jupiter – There goes Mars ---"

Miss Janey Conducted "Romper Room"", A complete television Kindergarten Weekday Mornings from 8;45 – 9:30 A.M. The children earned diplomas after two weeks on the show,,

This Photo shows the Personalities from WTAE-TV tobogganing at Seven Springs, Janey Vance, Jean, Connely, Eleanor Schano & Hank Stohl.

Janey Vance died unexpectedly in December of 1969.

Jan Bohna graciously stepped in to continue as hostess of "Romper room."

This photo shows the personalities from WTAE-TV tobogganing at Seven Springs.

Janey Vance, Jean, Connelly, Eleanor Schano & Hank Stohl

Photo Courtesy WTAE-TV

Joe Negri
(Handyman Negri)

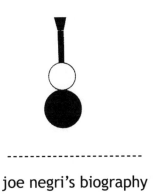

joe negri's biography

Joe is one of the most recognized names in Pittsburgh music circles and quite possibly one of the finest jazz guitarists in the country. He was a musical prodigy at age four, and was touring nationally by the age of sixteen. He has performed with such diverse performers as:

Johnny Mathis, Tony Bennett, Andy Williams,
Wynton, Branford and Ellis Marsalis, and YoYo Ma.

Joe Negri's career has spanned several decades and he has performed in every aspect of the music business. He appears frequently as a guest with the Pittsburgh Symphony and the Pittsburgh Symphony Pops with Marvin Hamlish. He's featured on the P.S.O.'s recording "Cinema Serenade" with Ishtak Pearlman and John Williams.

Joe served as 'musical director' at WTAE-TV. (the A.B.C. affiliate in Pittsburgh) for more than 20 years. While at WTAE, he produced and performed on several award winning T.V. programs. His frequent appearances as a Handyman Negri on the P.B.S. Mister Rogers Neighborhood Show had provided Negri with nationwide T.V., exposure. He has been a "key" performer on that show from its inception. The program continues to be a strong part of the PBS children's lineup.

Mr. Negri has also distinguished himself as a composer. He and humorist/writer Bob McCully have written and produced many musical revues. His composition "The Crossing" (for brass band and jazz trio) was premiered by The River City Brass Band. His most recent work "The Mass of Hope" (scored for mixed choir and jazz ensemble) has received critical and artistic acclaim.

Joe continues to lead an extremely active life as a musician. He also shares his knowledge and experience of jazz guitar through his teaching at Pitt, Duquesne, and his alma mater Carnegie Mellon University. In recent years Joe has been honored by many local organizations. In 1998 he was honored by both the Pittsburgh Cultural Trust and The Pittsburgh Italian Scholarship Fund. In 2000 Joe received the Mellon Jazz Community Award.

This year on April 1st Joe will receive a coveted "Elsie" award. Some previous awardees include Fred Rogers, Barbara Bush, Michael Keaton and others.

Joe resides in his favorite city Pittsburgh, with his wife Joni. They have three daughters and three granddaughters.

Hank Stohl

Joe Negri

WTAE TV Reunion Material

www.pbs.org/rogers
www.misterrogers.org

CHILDREN'S FAVORITES ON WTAE

JANEY VANCE...Miss Janey conducts "Romper Room's" complete television kindergarten weekday mornings from 8:45 to 9:30 A.M. Classes of six boys and girls earn diplomas after two weeks on the show.

RICKI WERTZ...Ricki and her dog Copper have continued as Pittsburgh's favorite morning children's show. A daily feature, Monday through Friday, from 9:30 to 10:00 A.M., the "Ricki and Copper" show plays host to

six children celebrating birthdays. The children participate and cartoons are featured.

HANK STOHL... Knish, Rodney and Connie entertain kids of all ages with Popeye cartoons and commentary on life in general, weekdays from 4:25 to 5:00 P.M. The program is entitled "Popeye 'n' Knish" and has long been a daily must for youngsters and parents alike.

PAUL SHANNON...features all the children's favorite comedies and cartoons, plus some very unusual guests on his "Adventure Time" program, weekday evenings at 5:00 P.M. The "3 Stooges" have been an integral part of Paul's show  for many years and new characters such as Nosmo King add greatly to the children's enjoyment.

Ricki Wertz, Copper, Nick Perry and Paul Shannon. at far right *unknown*

Backstage at the civic arena. Joe Negri, Ricki Wertz, Paul Shannon (Honorary Barker for The Evening) of WTAE at the circus, Janey Vance at far right. Picture courtesy Joe Negri, Zebra and Camel unnamed.

At a WTAE-TV Reunion, Henry DeBecco, Hank Stohl and Paul Shannon

Nickelodeon

Nickelodeon
1956

It was an hour long show on KDKA-TV, featuring the film shorts of Laurel and Hardy, hosted by Knish & Rodney, with an assist from Connie. from studio "B".

Legal Permission had to be granted to KDKA-TV, from Johnny Harris of the Harris family who still had rights to the Name, "Nickelodeon". The very first Nickelodeon in the country was on Penn Avenue in downtown Pittsburgh, founded by the Harris Family, circa 1905.

It cost a nickel in the early 1900's to see the very first silent films, thus the name, "Nickelodeon".

There are no Photos or files available on this program.

Oliver Hardy became very ill in North Hollywood, California ---

The children who watched the program sent 3,000 get well cards to Oliver Hardy, who died in 1957.

Hank Stohl gets approval from John Harris to use name "Nickelodeon" owned by the Harris Family.

Hank Stohl

1 Gateway Center, Pittsburgh 22, Pa.

presents

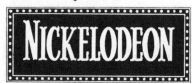

There's fun for both small-fry and adults on KDKA-TV's comedy series . . . timed for the after-school audience and featuring the famous Little Rascal films and Hank Stohl's puppets.

5:00 to 5:30 P.M. . . . Monday through Friday

The Program Nickelodeon, a half-hour show combining film and live talent, re-creates the atmosphere of an old-time movie house, with the famous Little Rascal comedy films and the unique talent of Hank Stohl and his fascinating puppets. Nickelodeon is a name with a special connotation for Pittsburgh where it was used to describe the world's first all-movie theatre.

The Talent Hank Stohl, creator and brains of KDKA-TV's "Knish" series, brings the original Nickelodeon Theatre back to the TV screen, as managed by his popular puppet, Rodney Hackenflash. Other puppets play the roles of candy butcher, usher, pianist, etc. Films shown star the well-known "Our Gang" characters—Spanky McFarland, Jackie Condon and others of this favorite comedy series which has been breaking popularity records since made available for television. While most of the films are in sound, some of the earlier silent episodes are narrated by Stohl.

Availability One-minute participations, film or limited live. Certain limited commercials, off-camera, can be delivered by Hank Stohl. See latest Rate Card.

Program prices subject to change without notice. Please confirm prices with KDKA-TV or Peters, Griffin, Woodward, Inc., before finalizing budget.

Represented by Peters, Griffin, Woodward, Inc.

Westinghouse Broadcasting Company, Inc.

Station Promotional Sales sheet for the show "Nickelodeon"

About the Author

Hank began his career in radio and experimental television as early as 1948, in Cincinnati, Ohio and Pittsburgh, Pennsylvania. Then to New York City to where he appeared in his highly successful children's TV Program,

As Creative director of his own creative company he also created several award winning radio and TV commercials as producer and writer for several National Accounts, Camel Cigarettes, International Industries, The island nation of Bermuda and Pepsi- West.

Hank also appeared in several series, and feature films, "Rockford files" ,"Highway to heaven", and "six million dollar man", along with appearances on "Days of our lives", and the Guiding light". His most recent film was "Diabolique' which starred Sharon Stone and Kathy Bates.

He is a published playwright and his two act comedy, "Lie a little" enjoyed great reviews while a member of the famed Masquers Club in Hollywood. Several one act plays have been published and produced Off-Off Broadway in New York.

Hank is married to Anita Heh, former staff member of the Pittsburgh Playhouse and musical comedy performer. They live in Stratford, Connecticut.